SCHOLASTIC

READING

SATs TESTS

YEAR 2

Published in the UK by Scholastic Education, 2019
Scholastic Distribution Centre, Bosworth Avenue, Tournament Fields,
Warwick, CV34 6UQ
Scholastic Ireland, 89E Lagan Road, Dublin Industrial Estate,
Glasnevin, Dublin, D11 HP5F
www.scholastic.co.uk
© 2019 Scholastic
456789 2345678901

A CIP catalogue record for this book is available from the British Library.
ISBN 978-1407-18303-9

Printed and bound by Ashford Colour Press

The book is made of materials from well-managed,
FSC®-certified forests and other controlled sources.

Author
Graham Fletcher

Series consultants
Lesley and Graham Fletcher

Editorial team
Rachel Morgan, Tracey Cowell, Anna Hall,
Helen Lewis, Shelley Welsh and Jane Jackson

Design team
Nicolle Thomas and Oxford Designers and Illustrators

Cover illustrations
Istock/calvindexter and Tomek.gr / Shutterstock/Visual Generation

Acknowledgements
Extracts from Department for Education website © Crown Copyright. Reproduced under the terms of the Open Government Licence
(OGL). www.nationalarchives.gov.uk/doc/open-government-licence/version/3/

Acknowledgements
The publishers gratefully acknowledge permission to reproduce the following copyright material:
Scoular Anderson c/o Caroline Sheldon Literary Agency Ltd. for the use of an extract from 'Backseat's Special Day' by Scoular
Anderson. Text © 1996, Scoular Anderson; Graham Fletcher for the use of 'How to write a party invitation'. Text © 2015, Graham
Fletcher. Holroyde Cartey Literary Agency for use of extracts and images from The Snow Lambs by Debi Gliori; Graham Fletcher for
the use of 'Floods', 'Norway', 'Trolls', 'Happy Valley Farm Visitor Centre', 'Hannah's helping hand', 'Little Boys', 'Wild weather', 'Oleg the
giant' and 'Oscars zoo'. Text © 2015, Graham Fletcher. Jenny Morris for the use of 'Weather at Work'. Text © 2015 Jenny Morris.
Every effort has been made to trace copyright holders for the works reproduced in this publication, and the publishers apologise for
any inadvertent omissions.

Illustrations: Moreno Chiacchiera, Beehive Illustration and Tomek.gr
Photographs:
Test A: © Stef Bennett/Shutterstock; © Heath Johnson/Shutterstock; © Air Images/ Shutterstock; © Pixeljoy/Shutterstock;
          © thieury/Shutterstock.
Test B: © Fotogenix/Shutterstock; © Yorkman/Shutterstock; © Matej Kastelic/Shutterstock; © Andrew Roland/Shutterstock;
          © Gorilla Images/Shutterstock; © Astudio/Shutterstock; © Perfect Lazybones/Shutterstock; © Brian Nolan/Shutterstock;
          © AuntSpray/Shutterstock; © Stockr/Shutterstock; © StudioSmart/Shutterstock; © Jaros/Shutterstock;
          © Mihai Simonia/Shutterstock.
Test C: © Zebra0209/Shutterstock; © Elmm/shutterstock; © Kjersti Joergensen/Shutterstock; © Sergey Bogomyako/Shutterstock;
          © Rob Kints/Shutterstock; © Anadman Bvba/Shutterstock; © Varuna/Shutterstock; © Nejron Photo/Shutterstock;
          With thanks to Les Scholes for permission to reproduce his illustrations for 'Oleg the Giant' and 'Oscar's Zoo' © 2015.

Contents
Reading: Year 2

About this book

This book provides you with practice papers to help support children with the Key Stage 1 Reading test.

Using the practice papers

The practice papers in this book can be used as you would any other practice materials. The children will need to be familiar with specific test-focused skills, such as reading carefully, leaving questions until the end if they seem too difficult, working at a suitable pace and checking through their work.

About the tests

Each Reading test has two papers:

- Paper 1: the reading text is mixed with questions. Children have about 30 minutes to read the text and answer the questions.

- Paper 2: there is a reading section containing a range of texts and a separate question section. Children have about 40 minutes to read all the texts and answer the questions. Children should refer back to the reading section for their answers.

Neither paper should be strictly timed. You should ensure that every child has enough time to demonstrate what he or she understands, knows and can do, without prolonging the test inappropriately. Use your judgement to decide when, or if, children need breaks during the assessment, and whether to stop the test early if appropriate.

The marks available for each question are shown in the test paper next to each question and are also shown next to each answer in the mark scheme. Incorrect answers do not get a mark and no half marks should be given.

There are three different types of answer.

- **Selected answers:** children may be required to choose an option from a list, draw lines to match answers, or tick a correct answer. Usually 1 mark will be awarded.

- **Short answers:** children will need to write a phrase from the text or use information from it. Usually 1 mark will be awarded.

- **Several line answers:** children will need to write a sentence or two. Usually 1–2 marks will be awarded.

- **Longer answers:** children will usually need to write more than one sentence using information from the text. Up to 2 marks will be awarded.

For Paper 1, a selection of 'useful words' are also provided. Discuss these words with your child before they start the test and make sure they understand them.

Advice for parents and carers

How this book will help

This book will support your child to get ready for the KS1 National Reading Tests. It provides valuable practice and help on the responses and content expected of Year 2 children aged 6–7 years.

In the weeks leading up to the National Tests, your child may be given plenty of practice, revision and tips to give them the best possible chance to demonstrate their knowledge and understanding. It is helpful to try to practise outside of school and many children benefit from extra input. This pack will help your child prepare and build their confidence.

In this book you will find three Reading tests. The layout and format of each test closely matches those used in the National Tests, so your child will become familiar with what to expect and get used to the style of the tests. There is a comprehensive answer section and guidance about how to mark the questions.

Tips

- Make sure that you allow your child to take the tests in a quiet environment where they are not likely to be interrupted or distracted.
- Make sure your child has a flat surface to work on, with plenty of space to spread out and good light.
- Emphasise the importance of reading and re-reading a question.
- These tests are similar to the ones your child will take in May in Year 2 and they therefore give you a good idea of strengths and areas for development. When you have found areas that require some more practice, it is useful to go over these again and practise similar types of question with your child.
- Go through the tests again together, identify any gaps in learning and address any misconceptions or areas of misunderstanding. If you are unsure of anything yourself, then make an appointment to see your child's teacher who will be able to help and advise further.
- Practising little and often will enable your child to build up confidence and skills over a period of time.

Advice for children

What to do before the test

- Revise and practise regularly.
- Spend some time each week practising.
- Focus on the areas you are less sure of to get better.
- Get a good night's sleep and eat a healthy breakfast.
- Be on time for school.
- Make sure you have all the things you need.

What to do in the test (paper 2)

- Read the texts to help you answer the questions.
- You may highlight, underline or make notes on the texts.
- You will have around 40 minutes to answer the questions.
- Make sure you read the instructions carefully.
- The marks for each question are shown on the right of each page.

Test coverage

Children will need to be able to:

- Use their knowledge of vocabulary to understand texts.
- Identify and explain key aspects of fiction and non-fiction including characters, titles, events and information.
- Identify and explain the sequence of events in texts.
- Make inferences from the text.
- Predict what might happen.

Introduction

- Read the text at the top of the page and then answer the questions.
- You may highlight, underline or make notes on the text.
- You will have around 30 minutes to answer all of the questions.
- Make sure you read the instructions carefully.
- The marks for each question are shown on the right of each page.
- Look at the useful words on page 8. Make sure you understand them. Discuss them with a teacher, parent or carer if you are not sure.
- There is a practice question on page 9.

Useful words

jog their memories

invitations

signature

hashtag

Backseat's Special Day

Backseat waited and waited. He was a very patient dog. He waited for days, he waited for months. He was waiting for his Special Day. Everyone else in the family had a Special Day.

Marks

Practice question

How long did Backseat wait for?

Circle **one**.

| hours | weeks | months | years |

1. How do you know Backseat was patient?

_____

_____   1

2. What was Backseat waiting for?

_____   1

On a Special Day you were given presents. You were spoiled. You were allowed to play special games and sing a special song called 'Happy Birthday to you!'.

Best of all, on your Special Day you were given lots and lots of special food, with a very big Special Day Cake.

3. Tick **all** the things that happen on a Special Day.

Marks

You are given presents. ☐

Your grandparents visit. ☐

You play special games. ☐

You have a special cake. ☐

You go to the park. ☐

1

That's why Backseat was waiting. He was quite sure that any day now it would be his turn to have a Special Day but it never came. Life went on. At home he lay around in all the wrong places, as usual.

In the car he was put right in the back seat, facing the opposite direction from everyone else, as usual. The family seemed to have forgotten about Backseat, so he would have to jog their memories. He decided to be very, *very* friendly.

---

4. In what ways was Backseat's life the same as usual?

Tick **two**.

Marks

He lay in all the wrong places. ☐

He sat in the back seat of the car. ☐

He decided to be very, *very* friendly. ☐

He would have to jog their memories. ☐

1

He tried to join the family at breakfast but he was told to go away.

When the children sat down on the sofa, Kate the cat always found a comfortable lap. Backseat decided to find a lap too but he was told to go away.

5. What happened when Backseat tried to remind the family about his Special Day?

Marks

_____

1

Backseat's plan wasn't working. Being extra friendly wasn't going to get him a Special Day. The family talked among themselves, stroked cats and read books about dinosaurs. They weren't interested in a dog.

Backseat had another plan. He would be very helpful. The family would have to give him a Special Day if he was a useful dog.

6. Tick **all** the things Backseat's family was doing instead of being interested in him.

reading ☐   eating ☐   talking ☐

feeding him ☐   sleeping ☐   stroking cats ☐

Marks

1

7. What was Backseat's new plan?

Tick **one**.

To do nothing ☐   To read books ☐

To be a useful dog ☐   To pretend to be a cat ☐

1

He soon got a chance. When a pencil case was lost he knew exactly where it was. He ran upstairs. He snuffled under the bed. He came back downstairs again... and popped the pencil case into the school bag.

Things didn't work out quite as he had planned. No one noticed that *he* had found the pencil case. They thought it had been in the bag all the time!

8. Find and **copy** the word that tells you how Backseat moved under the bed.

Marks

_____

_____

1

9. What happened when Backseat put the pencil case in the bag?

_____

_____

1

Think about everything you have read.

Marks

10. Number the events below from **1** to **4** to show the order in which they happen in the story.

Number 1 has been done for you.

Backseat was very helpful. ☐

Backseat sat in the back of the car. ☐

Backseat wanted a Special Day. 1

The family told Backseat to go away. ☐

1

Think about everything you have read.

Marks

11. What would be another good title for this story?
Tick **one**.

The Special Dog ◯   The Happy Dog ◯

The Sad Dog ◯   Pets ◯

1

12. Do you think Backseat will get his Special Day?
Explain why you think this.

_____

_____

1

How to write a party invitation

It's your birthday! Hooray! You are going to have a party. You'll need to write some invitations for your friends. This is how you do it.

First of all, you have to decide how many people are coming. Will you invite the whole class or just some special friends? This will tell you how many invitations you need to make.

If you ask the whole class, that is a lot of invitations to write. Perhaps you could do them on a laptop and print them instead.

13. What is the link between the number of people you invite and the number of invitations you need?

Marks

_____

_____

1

14. Why might you use a laptop for your invitations?

_____

1

Now you need to think about what to put in your invitations.

You need to write the person's name. That goes at the top. You need to tell them what the invitation is for. If you don't, they won't know why they are coming or what to wear.

Next you need to tell them where the party will be. If you don't, they won't know where to go! They also need to know what time the party starts and what time it ends. Don't forget to put your name on it!

15. Draw lines to match the invitation to what should be on it.

Marks

the person's name

what to wear

Invitation

where the party will be

what time the party starts

how to get there

1

16. Find and **copy two other** things that should be on the invitation.

1. _____

2. _____

2

17. Why do you need to put your name on it?

_____

1

SCHOLASTIC National Curriculum SATs Tests

That will give you something that looks like this:

Party invitation

Dear Jack,

Please come to my birthday party at
the Village Hall on Saturday, July 5th.
The party starts at 2 o'clock and will end
at 5 o'clock. There will be lots of games
and food. I do hope you can come.

Amelia

All you need to do now is plan the games and the food, and then get ready to have a great time.

Marks

18. What time does the party end?

Tick **one**.

2 o'clock ☐   3 o'clock ☐

4 o'clock ☐   5 o'clock ☐

1

19. The name *Amelia* is written as a:

Tick **one**.

label. ☐   signature. ☐

picture. ☐   hashtag. ☐

End of paper

1

Test A: Paper 1 Marks

Question	Focus	Possible marks	Actual marks
1	Identify/explain key aspects	1	
2	Identify/explain key aspects	1	
3	Identify/explain key aspects	1	
4	Identify/explain key aspects	1	
5	Identify/explain key aspects	1	
6	Identify/explain key aspects	1	
7	Identify/explain key aspects	1	
8	Knowledge of vocabulary	1	
9	Identify/explain key aspects	1	
10	Sequence of events	1	
11	Making inferences	1	
12	Predicting	1	
13	Making inferences	1	
14	Making inferences	1	
15	Identify/explain key aspects	1	
16	Identify/explain key aspects	2	
17	Making inferences	1	
18	Identify/explain key aspects	1	
19	Knowledge of vocabulary	1	
Total		**20**	

SCHOLASTIC National Curriculum SATs Tests

Test A: Paper 2

Enjoy a special day at

Happy Valley Farm
Visitor Centre

Cows

Cows are kept for the milk they produce. Most of the milk we drink comes from cows. We also get meat (beef) from cows. A female is called a cow and a male is called a bull. A cow drinks about 30 litres of water a day.

We have 50 cows. You'll be able to get up close to them, and you could even try milking one of them!

Sheep

Sheep are kept for their wool and for their meat. A female sheep is called a ewe and a male is called a ram. Sheep often live in hilly areas. They protect themselves from other animals by staying in large flocks. Baby sheep are called lambs.

Why not come and hold one of our little lambs?

In the large adventure play area:

- large climbing frame
- nets and ropes
- tunnels
- swings
- slides.

Pigs

Pigs give us meat, including ham, bacon and pork. They are very intelligent animals and learn quickly. They dislike the heat and roll in the mud to keep cool. They even like swimming! A pig will eat almost anything. Pigs can run a mile in 7 minutes.

Chickens

Female chickens are called hens. They lay eggs all through their lives. Hens need to have a nest, in which they can lay their eggs. They build their nests by first scratching a hole in the ground. Then they pick up twigs and leaves to put around the hole.

Come early and help us find the eggs!

Open daily: 9am to 5pm

Adults: £5.75
Children: £3.25
Family ticket: £16

Special events each day!

9am – Egg collecting

10am and 2pm – Feed the piglets

11am and 3pm – Love a lamb

1pm – Milk a cow

Every hour – Tractor rides

Have a happy day at

Happy Valley Farm Visitor Centre
Happy Valley Lane
Blacktown
Herefordshire
HY6 3UT
www.happyvalley.co.uk

Coming soon:

- wild deer
- horses
- meerkats
- the wildlife pond
- 4D cinema
- chairlift and sky ride.

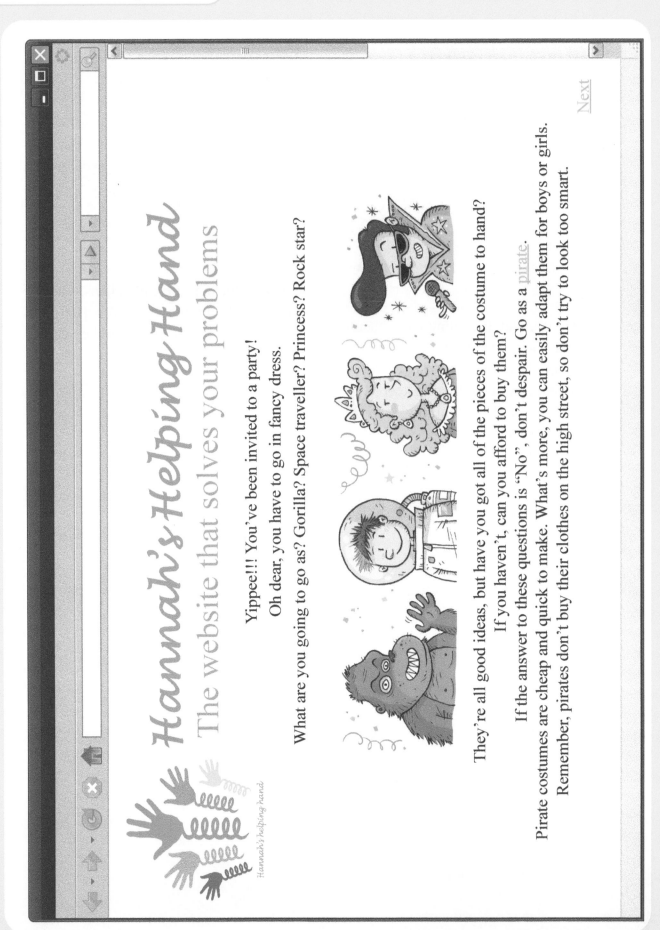

Hannah's Helping Hand
The website that solves your problems

Hannah's helping hand

Next

Yippee!!! You've been invited to a party!

Oh dear, you have to go in fancy dress.

What are you going to go as? Gorilla? Space traveller? Princess? Rock star?

They're all good ideas, but have you got all of the pieces of the costume to hand? If you haven't, can you afford to buy them? If the answer to these questions is "No", don't despair. Go as a pirate. Pirate costumes are cheap and quick to make. What's more, you can easily adapt them for boys or girls. Remember, pirates don't buy their clothes on the high street, so don't try to look too smart.

Hannah's helping hand

The website that solves your problems

A Pirate

Hannah's helping hand

Step 1: What you need
An old pair of jeans
An old T-shirt
A belt
Black boots
Black card
Scissors
Glue
Paint
String
A pirate picture

Step 2: The shirt
Cut off the T-shirt bottom and sleeves in a jagged pattern.
Use the paint to add stripes to your top.

Step 3: The trousers
Cut the legs off the jeans in a jagged pattern, half way between the knees and the ankles.

Step 4: The hat
Measure the distance round your head at ear level.
Draw a pirate's hat to fit your head, twice on a piece of card.
Cut out the pieces and glue them together.
Paint a skull and crossbones on the front.

Step 5: The extras
Add a belt over your T-shirt.
Wear the boots or go barefoot.
Draw an eye patch on a piece of card. Make a hole at each end of it. Thread string through the holes and tie it behind your head.
Make a cardboard sword and telescope. Put them in your belt.

Step 6: The finishing touches
Wear a bandana round your head instead of the pirate hat.
Wear a large earring.
Check your appearance in a mirror against your pirate picture.
Learn some pirate talk. *Shiver me timbers, me hearties, yer ready to walk the plank!*

LITTLE BOYS

Each Saturday as I grew up,
I tried to win the FA Cup.
With goals of jumpers in the park,
I'd play football till the dark.

My mother never let me play
A single game on a Sunday.
That day always went to plan,
As we would go to see my gran.

Now I am grown, it's not the same,
Old people never play a game.
And though it is less fun by far,
On Saturdays I wash the car.

On Sundays I rise, early morn,
And go outside to mow the lawn,
Then hope the afternoon's a grand one
As I await the visit of my grandson.

With goals of jumpers in the park,
We play football till the dark
And in his eyes, I sometimes see
The young boy who was little me.

Then sitting round the kitchen table,
He hears of times when I was able
To jump and skip and hop and run,
Back in the days when I was young.

Graham Fletcher (2015)

Marks

Questions 1–4 are about *Happy Valley Farm Visitor Centre* on pages **22–23**.

1. Circle the word that means the same as *special*. (page 22)

| usual | ordinary | normal | unusual |

1

2. Where do sheep often live? (page 22)

_____

1

3. At what time can you milk a cow? (page 23)

_____

1

4. Draw lines to match *Happy Valley Farm Visitor Centre* with reasons you might have a special day there. (pages 22–23)

| You can build a nest. |

| You will see lots of animals. |

Happy Valley Farm Visitor Centre

| You can go for free. |

| You can touch the animals. |

| You can watch a pig run a mile. |

1

Test A: Paper 2

Questions 5–9 are about *Hannah's helping hand* on pages **24–25**.

5. What does *Hannah's Helping Hand* website try to do? (page 24)

_____

_____

1

6.

> If the answer to these questions is "No", don't **despair**.

Draw a line to match the word *despair* to its meaning in this sentence. (page 24)

despair

bother

go

be happy

give up hope

give up trying

1

Marks

7. Why does the writer think that going to a fancy dress party in a pirate outfit is a good idea? (page 24)

Tick **one**.

It is cheap and quick to make. ☐

It is cheap. ☐

It is smart. ☐

It can be bought on the high street. ☐

1

8. Why do you need paint? (page 25)

Tick **one**.

To cut off the T-shirt bottom ☐

To draw the eye patch ☐

To add stripes to your top ☐

To colour the pirate picture ☐

1

9. What do you think will happen if you follow Hannah's instructions? (page 25)

_____

_____

1

Test A: Paper 2

Questions 10–18 are about *Little Boys* on page **26**.

Marks

10. Where did the writer try to win the FA Cup each Saturday? (page 26)

_____

_____

1

11. When did the writer never play football? (page 26)

Tick **one**.

When he was young ☐

On a Sunday ☐

In the dark ☐

Early in the morning ☐

1

12. What does the writer do on Saturdays now? (page 26)

Tick **one**.

Play football ☐   Wash the car ☐

Mow the lawn ☐   Tell stories ☐

1

13. Find and **copy one** line from the first verse that is repeated later in the poem. (page 26)

_____

_____

14. Give **two** reasons why the writer might look forward to his grandson's visits. (page 26)

1. _____

2. _____

15. Number these lines from the poem from **1** to **4** to show their order in the poem. (page 26)

Number 1 has been done for you.

Then sitting round the kitchen table ☐

On Sundays I rise, early morn ☐

I tried to win the FA Cup ☐ 1

We play football till the dark ☐

Marks

◯

1

◯

2

◯

1

Test A: Paper 2

Marks

16. Draw lines to match the rhyming words below. (page 26)

same	dark
plan	cup
up	game
park	gran

1

17. Give **two** reasons why the poem is called *Little Boys.* (page 26)

1. _____

2. _____

2

18. What would be another good title for the poem? (page 26)

Tick **one**.

The FA Cup ☐

Then and Now ☐

Old People ☐

My Grandson ☐

1

End of paper

Question	Focus	Possible marks	Actual marks
1	Knowledge of vocabulary	1	
2	Identify/explain key aspects	1	
3	Identify/explain key aspects	1	
4	Making inferences	1	
5	Identify/explain key aspects	1	
6	Knowledge of vocabulary	1	
7	Identify/explain key aspects	1	
8	Identify/explain key aspects	1	
9	Predicting	1	
10	Identify/explain key aspects	1	
11	Identify/explain key aspects	1	
12	Identify/explain key aspects	1	
13	Identify/explain key aspects	1	
14	Making inferences	2	
15	Sequence of events	1	
16	Knowledge of vocabulary	1	
17	Making inferences	2	
18	Making inferences	1	
Total		**20**	

Test B: Paper 1

Introduction

- Read the text at the top of the page and then answer the questions.
- You may highlight, underline or make notes on the text.
- You will have around 30 minutes to answer all of the questions.
- Make sure you read the instructions carefully.
- The marks for each question are shown on the right of each page.
- Look at the useful words on page 35. Make sure you understand them. Discuss them with a teacher, parent or carer if you are not sure.
- There is a practice question on page 36.

Useful words

elm

cocoon

brewing

flood defences

The Snow Lambs

By Debi Gliori

It was just before teatime when the snow started falling. Sam, his dad and Bess the sheepdog were counting in the sheep from the river field.

"I think you counted that sheep twice, Dad," said Sam.

Marks

Practice question

Bess is:

Tick **one**.

a sheepdog ☐   a sheep ☐

Sam's father ☐   Sam's mother ☐

1. When did the snow start falling?

_____

_____

1

2. Who was **not** counting in the sheep?

Tick **one**.

Mum ☐   Dad ☐   Bess ☐   Sam ☐

1

3. What might happen if Dad does not count the sheep properly?

_____

1

Dad was looking up at the sky where storm clouds gathered. The branches on the old elm creaked and Sam shivered. He looked around. I wonder where Bess is, he thought.

Marks

4. What could Dad see in the sky?

Tick **one**.

branches ☐

Sam shivering ☐

sheep ☐

clouds gathering ☐

1

5. | *I wonder where Bess is* |

What do these words tell you about Sam's feelings?

_____

1

"If the wind gets up, that old elm could blow down across the power lines, and we'd be in trouble," said Dad.

The wind felt full of sharp little teeth, nibbling at Sam's nose and biting his ears. "Come on, Sam, let's get these sheep in," said Dad.

"I can't see Bess anywhere," said Sam. "Where is she?"

When the sheep were safe inside, Dad yelled, "BESS! BESS, COME HERE!" His voice was lost in the wind.

Marks

6. What damage could the wind do?

_____

_____

1

7. Number the events below from 1 to 4 to show the order in which they happen.

Number 1 has been done for you.

Sam can't see Bess. ☐

Dad's voice is lost in the wind. ☐

Dad is worried about the wind. ☐ 1

The sheep are safe inside. ☐

1

"Come on Sam, let's get you inside – you look half-frozen," he said. They took off their boots and coats in the porch. Dad bolted the door behind them.

"But how will Bess get in?" asked Sam.
"She won't," said Dad. "That dog is useless. Maybe being shut out will teach her a lesson."

Marks

8. Why did Dad want Sam to come inside?

_____

_____

1

9. Draw lines to match Dad to his thoughts about Bess.

She is half-frozen.

She is useless.

Dad

She won't come home.

Being shut out will teach her a lesson.

1

After supper it was bathtime. As Sam jumped into his bath with a huge SPLASH, he thought, Bess will need a good hot bath when she gets in.

Mum wrapped Sam up in the cocoon of a warm towel, then dried his hair.

"That's quite a storm brewing out there," said Mum.

"Will Bess be blown away?" asked Sam.

"Don't worry, Sam. Bess can look after herself," replied Mum.

I hope Bess doesn't have to dig her way home, thought Sam, digging out his pyjamas.

10. How do you know it is colder outside the house than inside?

_____

_____

11. Find and **copy two** things that show that Sam is worried about Bess.

1. _____

2. _____

Marks

1

2

Sam wriggled into his pyjamas.

HELP! He thought, I can't see a thing.

Outside, snow filled the sky with blinding white flakes.

I hope Bess can find her way home, thought Sam.

12. Why did Sam think that Bess might find it difficult to find her way home?

Tick **one**.

Marks

He couldn't see her. ☐

She couldn't smell easily in the snow. ☐

The snow was blinding. ☐

She was lost. ☐

1

Sam asked Dad to read him a monster story, and then wished he hadn't. It was a very scary story. Outside the wind howled.

"I hope Bess isn't scared too," whispered Sam.

The wind grew louder, hurling itself at the house as if it wanted to tear the roof off.

"Bed's the safest place on a night like this," said Dad.

"No!" said Sam.

"Come on, Sam. Upstairs," said Mum.

"I'm not going," cried Sam. "I've got to wait up for Bess."

Marks

13. Think about all you have read.

Give one reason why you think Bess might come back.

_____

_____

1

14. What would be another good title for this story?

Tick **one**.

The Old Tree ◯   The Weather ◯

The Lost Dog ◯   Bathtime ◯

1

Floods

Britain has been having more floods than ever before. This is because there has been so much rain. In January 2014, there was more rain than there had ever been in one month before. Rivers were not able to take it all in. The waters rose and rivers burst their banks, flooding the land around.

15. What does *burst their banks* mean?

Tick **one**.

Marks

Water levels went down. ☐

Water levels stayed the same. ☐

Water went over the top. ☐

Water stopped moving. ☐

1

Flooding is dangerous. It causes a lot of damage, which costs a lot of money to put right. It can destroy homes and places of work. When this happens people have to move out and find somewhere else to live or work.

16. Draw lines to match flooding to what it does.

Marks

It causes a lot of damage.

It destroys homes.

Flooding

It saves people money.

It lets people live in their homes.

It makes people find other places to work.

1

In areas where flooding is known to happen a lot, some people move everything upstairs when the weather warnings say rain is coming. This can be a good idea, but the rain can be so heavy and the water so deep that the only way people can escape from their houses is by boat.

17. What is a weather warning?

Marks

_____

_____

1

Flood defences

It seems likely that we will carry on having very wet weather. In some places people are building flood defences to stop the rivers spilling their water. These defences are like walls or fences around the areas of the rivers that are likely to flood. Hopefully this will work, and people and buildings will be safe in the future.

Marks

18. Where are flood defences?

Tick **one**.

Around buildings ☐   Around rivers ☐

Around walls ☐   Around fences ☐

1

19. What do you think will happen if the flood defences do not work?

_____

_____

1

End of paper

Question	Focus	Possible marks	Actual marks
1	Identify/explain key aspects	1	
2	Identify/explain key aspects	1	
3	Predicting	1	
4	Identify/explain key aspects	1	
5	Making inferences	1	
6	Identify/explain key aspects	1	
7	Sequence of events	1	
8	Identify/explain key aspects	1	
9	Identify/explain key aspects	1	
10	Making inferences	1	
11	Making inferences	2	
12	Making inferences	1	
13	Making inferences	1	
14	Making inferences	1	
15	Knowledge of vocabulary	1	
16	Identify/explain key aspects	1	
17	Knowledge of vocabulary	1	
18	Identify/explain key aspects	1	
19	Predicting	1	
Total		**20**	

Test B: Paper 2

Wild Weather

In this country, we are very lucky because our weather is quite good. You might not think that on a cold day in January when there is snow on the ground, but it is true. We do get some bad weather, but it never lasts long.

Skiing in the Alps

Brr, it's cold!

Some places are very cold. The North Pole is almost freezing all year long. The large icebergs would not be there if it was warm. The South Pole is the same, but there are lots of places in the world that are cold for large parts of the year.

In France and Italy, the Alps are covered in snow for the whole winter. This is because they are very high. The higher you are, the colder it is. The colder it is, the more chance of snow there is. This is not a bad thing. Lots of people go to the Alps each winter to ski.

No it's not – it's hot!

Other places are very hot all year. India and most of Africa have lots of sunshine, but the sunniest place in the world is Arizona in America. It has over 4000 hours of sun each year.

Some places are both hot and cold. The Sahara Desert is roasting during the day, but freezing cold at night. This is because the clear skies let in the sun's heat in the day time, but they also let it out at night.

The Sahara Desert

It's not always good

Many people think that hot countries are great because of the heat. In those places it is always hot. There is nowhere to get away from the heat. It can make you very tired.

There is also a price to be paid for having it hot. Often countries that are hot are very dry and do not have enough water. Other hot countries have too much water. Some of them have 'monsoon' seasons. In these, there is very heavy rainfall every day for months. Some countries only have two seasons – a hot, dry one and a hot, wet one.

Monsoon rain in India

That wind is strong!

We get strong winds. What we don't get are hurricanes. These happen a lot in the Caribbean Sea. Very strong winds and rains attack some islands every year, causing lots of damage. They knock down buildings and make floods. Hurricanes sometimes miss the islands and head on towards the mainland of America, arriving in places like Florida and Texas, where lots of people go on holiday.

Damage caused by a hurricane

We did have a hurricane once in this country. In 1987, one hit the south coast. People did not expect it. It blew trees over and took the roofs off some houses. People were frightened by it. We were lucky because it was not a very large hurricane and it soon went away, but it still did a lot of damage.

Could it be worse?

Yes, it could! It may seem odd, but there is something worse than strong winds and rain. It's not really weather, though. It is called a *tsunami* (say 'soo-nar-mee'). A tsunami is a giant wave. It can be caused by an earthquake, a volcano or an explosion under the sea. This makes the sea rush towards the land very quickly. When it hits the shore it causes lots of damage. In 2004, a tsunami hit the whole of the Indian Ocean area. It swept away whole villages and killed many people.

Why don't we get wild weather?

We do not get much really bad weather in this country. This is because of where we are. We live on an island, so we have water all around us. This stops the temperature getting too cold or too hot. Also, warm water comes from the west and helps keep the temperature up. We do not have earthquakes or volcanoes, so we do not get tsunamis.

The weather is changing

Our seasons are getting more like each other. Winter is not as cold as it used to be, and summer is wetter. We would all like really hot summers and a white Christmas, but they are not happening as often as they used to.

Next time you think that our weather is bad, think about the other parts of the world and you will see that it's not so bad after all. It seems that our weather is getting warmer and wetter. The world has always had changing weather. We have had ice ages, when the whole earth was covered with a thick blanket of ice, and hotter times when everywhere was steamy. At present we are somewhere in the middle. Perhaps that's the best place to be.

Britain during the last Ice Age

Weather at Work

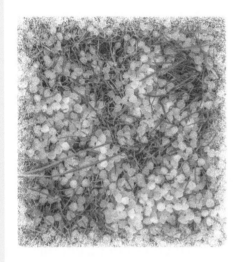

I'm a speeding hailstone,
An icy lump.

I'm a clap of thunder,
A noisy thump.

I'm a chilly snowflake,
Soft and white.

I'm a ray of sunshine,
Warm and bright.

I'm a falling raindrop,
Sploshing to the ground.

I'm a winter snowball,
Hard and round.

I'm a flash of lightning,
A magic sight.

You can see me zigzag,
Lighting up the night.

Jenny Morris

SCHOLASTIC National Curriculum SATs Tests

Marks

Questions 1–14 are about *Wild Weather* on pages **49–51**.

1. Why are we lucky in this country? (page 49)

Tick **one**.

Our weather is wild. ☐   Our weather is quite good. ☐

It snows in January. ☐   We get some bad weather. ☐

1

2. Why wouldn't there be icebergs near the North Pole if it was warm? (page 49)

Tick **one**.

They would sink. ☐   They would melt. ☐

They would float to the South Pole. ☐   They would freeze together. ☐

1

3. Why are the Alps covered in snow for most of the winter? (page 49)

_____

_____

1

4. Where is the sunniest place in the world? (page 49)

_____

1

5. What makes the Sahara Desert hot in the day and cold at night? (page 49)

Marks

Tick **one**.

Clear skies ☐   The sun ☐

The dark ☐   The light ☐

1

6. Draw lines to link *hot countries* to their problems. (page 50)

| hot countries |

Not enough water

Not enough shade

Too much shade

Too many seasons

Too much water

1

7. What is a monsoon season? (page 50)

_____

_____

2

8.

> *Very strong winds and rains **attack** some islands every year, causing lots of damage.*

What does the word *attack* tell you about the winds and rains? (page 50)

_____

1

9. Why is a *tsunami* **not** wild weather? (page 51)

Marks

Tick **one**.

It is an earthquake. ☐

It is a giant wave. ☐

It is an underwater explosion. ☐

It is a volcano. ☐

1

10. What do waters from the west do to our weather? (page 51)

_____

1

11. Draw lines to match *our weather* to how the seasons are changing. (page 51)

| Summers are getting wetter. |
| Winters are getting colder. |
| Winters are getting longer. |
| Winters are getting less cold. |
| Summers are getting drier. |

our weather

1

12. What happens in ice ages? (page 51)

Tick **one**.

The Earth melts. ☐

The Earth freezes. ☐

The Earth steams. ☐

The Earth floods. ☐

Marks

1

13. How do you think our weather will change in the future? Why do you think this? (page 51)

_____

_____

_____

1

14. Why is *Wild Weather* a good title for this piece? (page 51)

_____

1

Marks

Questions 15–19 are about *Weather at Work* on page **52**.

15. Find and **copy one** word from the poem that means the same as *cold*. (page 52)

_____

_____

1

16. Which kind of weather is *a noisy thump*? (page 52)

_____

_____

1

17. Which word means the same as *sploshing*? (page 52)

Tick **one**.

Splattering ☐

Falling ☐

Drowning ☐

Twirling ☐

1

18. Circle the **four** words that rhyme. (page 52)

Marks

| night | ground | bright |

| white | lump | sight |

1

---

19. Number the phrases below from **1** to **4** to show the order in which they appear in the poem.

Number 1 has been done for you. (page 52)

A flash of lightning ☐

A falling raindrop ☐

A winter snowball ☐

A ray of sunshine ☐ 1

1

End of paper

Question	Focus	Possible marks	Actual marks
1	Identify/explain key aspects	1	
2	Making inferences	1	
3	Identify/explain key aspects	1	
4	Identify/explain key aspects	1	
5	Identify/explain key aspects	1	
6	Identify/explain key aspects	1	
7	Identify/explain key aspects	2	
8	Knowledge of vocabulary	1	
9	Identify/explain key aspects	1	
10	Identify/explain key aspects	1	
11	Identify/explain key aspects	1	
12	Making inferences	1	
13	Predicting	1	
14	Making inferences	1	
15	Knowledge of vocabulary	1	
16	Identify/explain key aspects	1	
17	Knowledge of vocabulary	1	
18	Knowledge of vocabulary	1	
19	Sequence of events	1	
Total		**20**	

Introduction

- Read the text at the top of the page and then answer the questions.
- You may highlight, underline or make notes on the text.
- You will have around 30 minutes to answer all of the questions.
- Make sure you read the instructions carefully.
- The marks for each question are shown on the right of each page.
- Look at the useful words on page 61. Make sure you understand them. Discuss them with a teacher, parent or carer if you are not sure.
- There is a practice question on page 62.

Useful words

61

fjords

inlets

valuable

cunning

Test C: Paper 1

Norway

Norway is a beautiful country. It has many mountains, lakes and rivers. One side of Norway borders the sea and it has a very long coast, so it is not a surprise that many Norwegians are good sailors.

Marks

Practice question

Why are many people from Norway good sailors?

Tick **two**.

Norway has many mountains. ☐

Norway has a very long coast. ☐

One side of Norway borders the sea. ☐

Norway is beautiful. ☐

1. Norway is:

Tick **one**.

a country ☐   an island ☐

a mountain ☐   a lake ☐

1

2. What are people who live in Norway called?

_____

1

Vikings came to Britain in longships like this.

Hundreds of years ago, Vikings came from Norway to Britain. At first they came to steal, but later they stayed and lived here. They took lots of land and even the city of York, which they called Jorvik. Today you can see how the Vikings lived by going to the Jorvik Viking Centre in York.

Marks

3. Which city was taken by the Vikings?

_____

_____

1

4. Where can you see how Vikings lived?

Tick **one**.

Vikings ☐   Norway ☐

London ☐   Jorvik Viking Centre ☐

1

Norway is a long way north. The days and nights are not like they are in Britain. In the summer, most parts of Norway have daylight for over twenty hours each day and in the very far north, the sun does not really go down at all. In the winter, there are very few daylight hours and the sun is hardly seen in the north. This means that it has very cold winters.

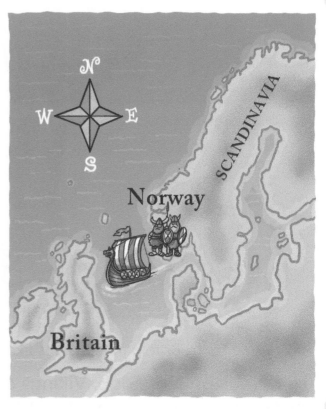

5. Where is Norway?

_____

_____

Marks

1

6. Why does Norway have very cold winters?

Tick **one**.

The days and nights are not like they are in Britain. ☐

It has over twenty hours of daylight every day. ☐

The sun does not really go down at all. ☐

There are very few daylight hours. ☐

1

Whales and basking sharks swim in the waters around Norway. On the land, there are brown bears. On one of the northern islands there are even polar bears. Perhaps that is why the Vikings liked Britain!

Marks

7. Which animals swim in the waters around Norway?

Tick **two**.

Whales ☐   Polar bears ☐

Basking sharks ☐   Brown bears ☐

1

8. Why might the Vikings have liked Britain?

_____

_____

1

Test C: Paper 1

Norway is famous for its fjords. These are long, narrow inlets from the sea. They have very steep sides. They were made long ago by glaciers. The glaciers cut into the land. When the glaciers moved back, they left long, narrow, deep waterways.

Marks

9. Norway is famous for:

Tick **one**.

its fjords ☐   its sea ☐

its sides ☐   its sheets of ice ☐

1

10. Draw lines to match fjords to **three** facts about them.

They are long, narrow inlets from the sea.

They are not very deep.

Fjords

They have steep sides.

They were made by glaciers.

They are lakes.

1

Today Norway is a modern country. Its people are friendly and do not like fighting. Many people go to Norway for holidays. Sometimes they go to see the beautiful lakes  and mountains; sometimes they go to see the fjords; sometimes they go to ski on the mountains in the winter. People go to Norway for many reasons, but they are all very glad that they have been, and come home wanting to go back again.

11. Why do many people go to Norway?
Tick **one**.

It is a modern country. ☐   To fight ☐

For holidays ☐   It is hot ☐

Marks

1

12. Why might people want to go back to Norway?
Circle **two** reasons.

It is a modern country.

It is a beautiful country.

Its people do not like fighting.

There are many things to see and do.

1

Trolls

In the myths and legends of countries like Norway and Sweden, trolls were powerful monsters. They were tough, ugly creatures with a hard, rock-like skin. They had small, beady eyes and large, bumpy noses. Most trolls looked very much like humans. Some of them were smaller or larger than ordinary people, but all of them were ugly and stupid. They lived in families in rocks and caves, under tree roots, or high in the mountains. They did not like humans, and many people thought they were dangerous.

Marks

13. Which words tell you that the stories about trolls are not true?

_____

_____

1

14. Why might people have thought trolls were dangerous?

_____

1

In the earliest stories, trolls only came out at night and were turned into stone by sunlight. In one legend, two great armies of trolls fought each other in a terrible battle. Neither side won because the sunrise caught them and they all changed into rocks.

15. Why would trolls fear sunrise?

Tick **one**.

They only came out at night. ☐

The sun turned them into stone. ☐

The sun blinded them. ☐

The sun made them want to fight other trolls. ☐

Marks

1

16. Which word makes the battle seem very bad?

_____

1

Many people thought that trolls stole large amounts of gold and silver, and that each troll had a huge pile of treasure. That meant that catching a troll would be a very good thing. But catching trolls wasn't enough. They had to be tricked into telling people where their treasure was hidden. Perhaps this was why trolls did not like humans.

17. Draw lines to match trolls to **two** things they stole.

Marks

gold

tricks

Trolls

silver

good things

1

It seems that the main reason for the stories about trolls was to let heroes win valuable prizes. The trolls were there to make the heroes look good. In return for defeating a troll by being brave and clever, the hero was rewarded with the troll's treasure, the king's daughter, castles and huge amounts of land.

Even nowadays trolls are popular in films and stories. They appear in *The Hobbit* and in some of the Harry Potter stories.

18. Find and **copy two** things heroes might get for defeating a troll, apart from the troll's treasure.

Marks

1. _____

2. _____

2

Are trolls real? It is unlikely, as they only seem to appear in stories. However, if you should be the first person to meet one, you had better be well prepared. You need to be brave, smart and strong. You'll need all of your wits and cunning. If none of that works, you'll have to hope for terrible weather, as it is believed that lightning frightens trolls away!

19. Why do you have to hope for terrible weather if you meet a troll?

Marks

_____

_____

1

End of paper

Question	Focus	Possible marks	Actual marks
1	Identify/explain key aspects	1	
2	Making inferences	1	
3	Identify/explain key aspects	1	
4	Identify/explain key aspects	1	
5	Identify/explain key aspects	1	
6	Making inferences	1	
7	Identify/explain key aspects	1	
8	Making inferences	1	
9	Identify/explain key aspects	1	
10	Identify/explain key aspects	1	
11	Identify/explain key aspects	1	
12	Making inferences	1	
13	Knowledge of vocabulary	1	
14	Making inferences	1	
15	Making inferences	1	
16	Knowledge of vocabulary	1	
17	Identify/explain key aspects	1	
18	Identify/explain key aspects	2	
19	Identify/explain key aspects	1	
	Total	20	

Test C: Paper 2

OLEG THE GIANT

At four feet eleven inches, Oleg was a giant. Four feet eleven inches may not be very tall in your world, but it was in Oleg's. He was not the biggest giant in his world, but he would be when he was fully grown.

Oleg lived next to his village. All the giants in Oleg's world had a village and this one was his. Oleg had lived there all his life, but something was not quite right about it.

When he was very young, Oleg had played with the village children, but as he had grown, he had become too big for them. He didn't fit into the park any more. He didn't fit into his house. He didn't fit into his clothes.

In fact, Oleg just didn't fit in at all.

When the village children didn't call for him to play any more, Oleg just sat alone outside the village and cried.

You might know someone like Oleg. You might be like Oleg. You might understand him. If you did, you could explain to him that it's all right not to fit in. Oleg might not understand though, because Oleg didn't understand himself.

The villagers did not like it when Oleg cried. The tears dripped down his nose and onto the ground, forming huge lakes. The rivers overflowed and flooded the streets. Some of the houses were swept away with the tide, sometimes with their owners still in them.

Oleg did not want to cause the villagers any harm. After all, he was their giant and they were his villagers, so he asked his mother what to do. She gave him a blanket to dry his eyes. This worked well until it got soaked. Oleg squeezed the blanket to wring it out, but the villagers complained that it was like a thunderstorm. That just made Oleg cry some more.

So Oleg sat on the hill outside the village by himself. Sometimes he cried and the villagers moaned. Sometimes he sighed and the villagers groaned.

The Lord Mayor knew that he had to talk to Oleg. The people in the next village were complaining now. This had all gone far enough, and he had to put a stop to it.

Oleg had cried so much that the entire area around the hill was a lake. He would have been up to his ankles in water if he had not sat on top of the hill.

Ankle deep may not be very deep in your world, but it was in Oleg's.

The Lord Mayor called for the navy to take him to Oleg. Unfortunately, the village was miles from the sea, so it didn't have a navy.

Was the Lord Mayor bothered by the lack of a navy? No, not a bit. He just invented one and made himself the High Sea Lord.

The Lord Mayor rowed across the lake. It was so new it didn't have a name, so the Lord Mayor named it after himself. So, the Lord Mayor rowed across Lord Mayor Lake to see Oleg.

"The villagers are ashamed of you," said the Lord Mayor.

Oleg was ashamed of himself. He sobbed and the Lord Mayor put up an umbrella to avoid being drenched. He was not going to give up. A little bit of water wasn't going to stop him!

He peeped out from under the umbrella and was caught full in the face by a teardrop that knocked him over and sank the boat.

The Lord Mayor wasn't the Lord Mayor for nothing. He was good at everything. He swam to the upturned umbrella and climbed into that.

"The people are fed up with you," he said. "All the other villages have real giants. We are a laughing stock. Why can't you be a real giant and do what real giants do?"

Oleg was ashamed. He wanted to be a real giant.

"We want a proper giant like all the other villages have."

Oleg was more ashamed. He didn't know what proper giants did. He was only a little giant.

"Proper giants *RAAAH* a lot and terrify their villagers. Proper giants are horrible and fearsome. Proper giants eat cows and rip up trees."

Oleg hadn't got any *RAAAH* in him. He didn't want to be horrible and fearsome. He didn't fancy eating cows. He liked beans more.

"You're our giant. Either be the giant we want or go somewhere else!"

Oleg was even more ashamed. They were his villagers and he was their giant, but he couldn't be the giant they wanted. It just wasn't in him, so he pulled himself up to his pathetic four feet eleven inches, turned sadly and sloshed away through the ankle-deep water, sinking the Lord Mayor's umbrella in a tidal wave behind him.

So Oleg left his problems behind him, but you know that's not the end, don't you? Sometimes what we think we want isn't what we really want at all. But you knew that, didn't you? If you knew Oleg, you might have told him.

Oscar's Zoo

Some zoos are large, some zoos are small,
but Oscar's Zoo takes up no space at all.
Tucked up each night in his jungle bed,
his zoo fills the dreams inside Oscar's head.

What strange animals can be found in its grounds?
What marvellous beasts, what wonderful sounds?

An Alliphant and an Elegator
Squashed into the elevator.
A Wallabear and Koalaby
Perched together in a tree.

There are ants in pants and some in skirts,
Goats in coats on top of their shirts,
Crocs in socks, a bat in a hat,
Gnus in shoes, well fancy all that!

Every night is an animals' feast
and all are included from greatest to least.
They mingle, they mutter, they squeak and
they squawk.
They jingle, they flutter and some even talk!

As he slumbers each night, clutching his teddy,
Oscar's Zoo is open, waiting and ready.
But every dawn, as night turns to day,
the zoo closes its gates and then fades away.

As Oscar wakes up, stretching and yawning,
his zoo disappears and is gone in the morning.
Oscar's Zoo is a secret, of which nothing is said,
known only to Oscar, to me, you and Ted.

Graham Fletcher (2015)

Marks

Questions 1–14 are about *Oleg the Giant* on pages **75–77**.

1. How do you know Oleg does not live in your world? (page 75)

_____

_____

1

2. Where did Oleg live? (page 75)

_____

_____

1

3. Circle the **three** things Oleg didn't fit into any more. (page 75)

the school   the park   the village

his house   his clothes

1

4. Why did Oleg's mother give him a blanket? (page 75)

Tick **one**.

To keep him warm ☐

To dry his eyes ☐

To make him go away ☐

To make a thunderstorm ☐

1

Marks

5.

> *So Oleg sat on the hill outside the village by himself.*
> *Sometimes he cried and the villagers moaned.*
> *Sometimes he sighed and the villagers groaned.*
> (page 76)

Draw lines to match the words that rhyme.

hill	sighed
cried	he
Oleg	moaned
groaned	villagers

1

6. Why did the Lord Mayor have to talk to Oleg? (page 76)

Tick **one**.

The Lord Mayor was
an important person. ☐

Oleg's tears had
made a lake. ☐

The people in the next
village were complaining. ☐

Oleg was up to his
ankles in the water. ☐

1

7. Why do you think the Lord Mayor named the lake after himself? (page 76)

Give **two** reasons.

1. _____

2. _____

2

8. What was the Lord Mayor good at? (page 77)

Tick **one**.

Nothing ☐   Climbing ☐

Everything ☐   Swimming ☐

Marks

1

---

9. Draw lines to match *Proper giants* with what they do. (page 77)

RAAAH a lot

terrify their villagers

Proper giants

fear some things

eat cows

plant trees

1

---

10. Which word means the same as *sloshed*? (page 77)

Tick **one**.

swam ☐   walked ☐

jumped ☐   splashed ☐

1

Test C: Paper 2

Marks

11. What sank the Lord Mayor's umbrella? (page 77)

_____

_____

1

12. Which of these is at the beginning **and** the end of the story? (page 75 and page 77)

Tick **one**.

Four feet eleven inches ◯   RAAAH ◯

The Lord Mayor ◯   Oleg's house ◯

1

13. At the end of the story, it says:

> *If you knew Oleg, you might have told him.*
> (page 77)

From all that you have read, what do you think the writer would want you to tell Oleg?

_____

_____

1

14. This is not the end of the story. What do you think will happen next?

_____

_____

1

Questions 15–19 are about *Oscar's Zoo* on page **78**.

Marks

15. Where is Oscar's Zoo? (page 78)

_____

_____

1

16. Circle the **two** animals that make up the Alliphant and the Elegator. (page 78)

koala bear and wallaby

goat and crocodile

alligator and elephant

ant and gnu

1

17. Look at the verse beginning,

Every night is an animals' feast (page 78)

Find and **copy two** noises the animals make.

1. _____

2. _____

1

Test C: Paper 2

18. Number the events below from **1** to **4** to show the order in which they happen.

Number 1 has been done for you.

Marks

Oscar goes to sleep.
| 1 |

Oscar's Zoo disappears.
| |

The animals have a feast.
| |

The Wallabear and Koalaby are in a tree.
| |

1

19. In the last line, who is *me*? (page 78)

_____

1

End of paper

Test C: Paper 2 Marks

Question	Focus	Possible marks	Actual marks
1	Identify/explain key aspects	1	
2	Identify/explain key aspects	1	
3	Identify/explain key aspects	1	
4	Identify/explain key aspects	1	
5	Knowledge of vocabulary	1	
6	Identify/explain key aspects	1	
7	Making inferences	2	
8	Identify/explain key aspects	1	
9	Identify/explain key aspects	1	
10	Knowledge of vocabulary	1	
11	Identify/explain key aspects	1	
12	Identify/explain key aspects	1	
13	Making inferences	1	
14	Predicting	1	
15	Identify/explain key aspects	1	
16	Making inferences	1	
17	Identify/explain key aspects	1	
18	Sequence of events	1	
19	Making inferences	1	
Total		**20**	

Marking and assessing the papers

The mark schemes provide detailed examples of correct answers (although other variations/phrasings are often acceptable) and an explanation about what the answer should contain to be awarded a mark or marks.

Although the mark scheme sometimes contains alternative suggestions for correct answers, some children may find other ways of expressing a correct answer. When marking these tests, exercise judgement when assessing the accuracy or relevance of an answer and give credit for correct responses.

Marks table

At the end of each test there is a table for you to insert the number of marks achieved for each question. This will enable you to see which areas your child needs to practise further.

National standard in Reading

The mark that your child gets in the test paper will be known as the 'raw score' (for example, '22' in 22/40). The raw score will be converted to a scaled score and children achieving a scaled score of 100 or more will achieve the national standard in that subject. These 'scaled scores' enable results to be reported consistently year-on-year.

The guidance in the table below shows the marks that children need to achieve to reach the national standard. This should be treated as a guide only, as the number of marks may vary. You can also find up-to-date information about scaled scores on our website: www.scholastic.co.uk/nationaltests

Marks achieved	Standard
0–24	Has not met the national standard in Reading for Key Stage 1
25–40	Has met the national standard in Reading for Key Stage 1

Mark scheme for Test A: Paper 1 (pages 7–20)

Q	Answers	Marks
	Practice question: months	
1	**Award 1 mark** for any one of the following: • Backseat waited and waited. • He was a very patient dog. • He waited for days, he waited for months. Or a summary, such as: *Backseat waited a long time for his Special Day.*	1
2	**Award 1 mark** for his Special Day	1
3	**Award 1 mark** for all three answers correct: You are given presents. You play special games. You have a special cake.	1
4	**Award 1 mark** for both answers correct: • He lay in all the wrong places. • He sat in the back seat of the car.	1
5	**Award 1 mark** for he was told to go away.	1
6	**Award 1 mark** for all three answers correct: reading, talking, stroking cats	1
7	**Award 1 mark** for: to be a useful dog	1
8	**Award 1 mark** for snuffled	1
9	**Award 1 mark** for either of the following: No one noticed that *he* had found the pencil case. Or: They thought it had been in the bag all the time!	1
10	**Award 1 mark** for all three correct: Backseat was very helpful. 4 Backseat sat in the back of the car. 2 Backseat wanted a Special Day. 1 The family told Backseat to go away. 3	1
11	**Award 1 mark** for: The Sad Dog	1
12	**Award 1 mark** for any plausible answer that includes a reason, such as: Yes, because Backseat will keep on finding ways to remind the family. No, because the family will continue to ignore him.	1
13	**Award 1 mark** for the number is the same or similar.	1
14	**Award 1 mark** for It is a lot to write by hand or You can print them out or similar.	1
15	**Award 1 mark** for all three answers correct: the person's name; where the party will be; what time the party starts	1
16	**Award 1 mark** for each of the following, in either order: 1. what the invitation is for 2. what time it ends	2
17	**Award 1 mark** for so people know who has sent it or similar.	1
18	**Award 1 mark** for: 5 o'clock	1
19	**Award 1 mark** for: signature	1

Mark scheme for Test A: Paper 2 (pages 21–33)

Q	Answers	Marks
1	**Award 1 mark** for: unusual	1
2	**Award 1 mark** for on hilly ground/in hilly areas	1
3	**Award 1 mark** for 1pm	1
4	**Award 1 mark** for both answers correct.	1

Happy Valley Farm Visitor Centre → You will see lots of animals.

Happy Valley Farm Visitor Centre → You can touch the animals.

Q	Answers	Marks
5	**Award 1 mark** for solve your problems, or similar.	1
6	**Award 1 mark** for: give up hope	1
7	**Award 1 mark** for: It is cheap and quick to make.	1
8	**Award 1 mark** for: To add stripes to your top	1
9	**Award 1 mark** for You will have a really good pirate costume, or similar.	1
10	**Award 1 mark** for (in) the park	1
11	**Award 1 mark** for: On a Sunday	1
12	**Award 1 mark** for: Wash the car	1
13	**Award 1 mark** for: With goals of jumpers in the park	1
14	**Award 1 mark** for each plausible reason based on the text, up to a maximum of **2 marks**, such as: • They play football. • He remembers what it was like to be young. • He gets to tell stories of when he was young.	2
15	**Award 1 mark** for all numbers correct. Then sitting round the kitchen table ④ I tried to win the FA Cup ① On Sundays I rise, early morn ② We play football till the dark ③	1
16	**Award 1 mark** for all pairs of rhyming words correctly matched. same – game plan – gran up – cup park – dark	1
17	**Award 1 mark** for each plausible explanation, up to a maximum of **2 marks**, such as: • It is about the grandfather when he was a little boy and his grandson who is a little boy. • It is about the things that little boys do. • It is a good summary of the poem.	2
18	**Award 1 mark** for: Then and Now	1

SCHOLASTIC National Curriculum SATs Tests

Q	Answers	Marks
	Practice question: a sheepdog	
1	**Award 1 mark** for Just before teatime **Do not accept**: before teatime or teatime.	1
2	**Award 1 mark** for: Mum	1
3	**Award 1 mark** for he might not get them all in safely, or similar.	1
4	**Award 1 mark** for: clouds gathering	1
5	**Award 1 mark** for he was worried about where Bess was, or similar.	1
6	**Award 1 mark** for (The wind could) blow down the old elm (onto the power lines).	1
7	**Award 1 mark** for all numbers correct. Sam can't see Bess. 2 Dad's voice is lost in the wind. 4 Dad is worried about the wind. 1 The sheep are safe inside. 3	1
8	**Award 1 mark** for He looked half-frozen, He was very cold, or similar.	1
9	**Award 1 mark** for both lines drawn correctly to: ● She is useless. ● Being shut out will teach her a lesson.	1
10	**Award 1 mark** for: There is a storm outside but it is warm inside, or similar.	1
11	**Award 1 mark** for each of the following, up to a maximum of **2 marks**: ● Bess will need a good hot bath when she gets in. ● Will Bess be blown away? ● I hope Bess doesn't have to dig her way home.	2
12	**Award 1 mark** for: The snow was blinding.	1
13	**Award 1 mark** for any plausible explanation for Bess's return; for example: ● She could use her sense of smell to find her way back. ● The weather might improve. ● The story doesn't say she is hurt. ● It would give the story a happy ending. ● Sam is going to wait up until she comes home. ● Bess loves Sam.	1
14	**Award 1 mark** for: The Lost Dog	1
15	**Award 1 mark** for: Water went over the top.	1
16	**Award 1 mark** for all three lines drawn correctly to: ● It causes a lot of damage. ● It destroys homes. ● It makes people find other places to work.	1

Q	Answers	Marks
17	**Award 1 mark** for any clear explanation, such as: • It tells people the weather will be bad. • It tells people rain is coming. • It tells people that floods might happen.	1
18	**Award 1 mark** for: Around rivers	1
19	**Award 1 mark** for any plausible suggestion of what might happen, such as: • Rivers will continue to flood. • Damage will continue to happen. • People and buildings will not be safe.	1

Mark scheme for Test B: Paper 2 (pages 48–59)

Q	Answers	Marks
1	**Award 1 mark** for: Our weather is quite good.	1
2	**Award 1 mark** for: They would melt.	1
3	**Award 1 mark** for They are very high.	1
4	**Award 1 mark** for Arizona (in America) **Do not accept**: (in) America.	1
5	**Award 1 mark** for: Clear skies	1
6	**Award 1 mark** for both lines drawn correctly to: • Not enough water • Too much water	1
7	**Award 2 marks** for: A time when there is very heavy rainfall for months, or similar. **Award 1 mark** for: Answers that only refer to heavy rain but do not include the amount of time.	2
8	**Award 1 mark** for any answer that refers to the strength or violence of the wind and rain.	1
9	**Award 1 mark** for: It is a giant wave.	1
10	**Award 1 mark** for keep the temperature up, or similar.	1
11	**Award 1 mark** for both lines drawn correctly to: • Summers are getting wetter. • Winters are getting less cold.	1
12	**Award 1 mark** for: The Earth freezes.	1
13	**Award 1 mark** for any answer that gives a reason for future climate change, such as: • It will continue to get warmer and wetter because that seems to be the way it is going. • It will get colder because we have not had an ice age for a long time. • Do not accept any answer that describes future climate change without giving a reason.	1
14	**Award 1 mark** for any answer that explains why the title is suitable, such as: • It tells you what the text is all about. • It is a summary of the text.	1
15	**Award 1 mark** for icy or chilly	1
16	**Award 1 mark** for a clap of thunder	1
17	**Award 1 mark** for: Splattering	1
18	**Award 1 mark** for all four words correct: night, bright, white, sight	1

Q	Answers	Marks
19	**Award 1 mark** for all numbers correct. a flash of lightning 4 a falling raindrop 2 a winter snowball 3 a ray of sunshine 1	1

Mark scheme for Test C: Paper 1 (pages 60–73)

Q	Answers	Marks
	Practice question: Norway has a very long coast. One side of Norway borders the sea.	
1	**Award 1 mark** for: a country	1
2	**Award 1 mark** for: Norwegians	1
3	**Award 1 mark** for: York	1
4	**Award 1 mark** for: Jorvik Viking Centre	1
5	**Award 1 mark** for: a long way north	1
6	**Award 1 mark** for: There are very few daylight hours.	1
7	**Award 1 mark** for both answers correct: • Whales • Basking sharks	1
8	**Award 1 mark** for: there were no sharks / brown bears / polar bears / dangerous animals, or similar.	1
9	**Award 1 mark** for: its fjords	1
10	**Award 1 mark** for all three answers correct: • They are long, narrow inlets from the sea. • They have steep sides. • They were made by glaciers.	1
11	**Award 1 mark** for: For holidays	1
12	**Award 1 mark** for both answers correct: • It is a beautiful country. • There are many things to see and do.	1
13	**Award 1 mark** for: myths and legends	1
14	**Award 1 mark** for: they did not like humans so might hurt them, or similar.	1
15	**Award 1 mark** for: The sun turned them into stone.	1
16	**Award 1 mark** for: terrible	1
17	**Award 1 mark** for both answers correct: • gold • silver	1
18	**Award 1 mark** for each of the following, up to a maximum of **2 marks**: • the king's daughter • huge amounts of land • castles • valuable prizes	2
19	**Award 1 mark** for: lightning frightens trolls away, or similar.	1

Mark scheme for Test C: Paper 2 (pages 74–85)

Q	Answers	Marks
1	**Award 1 mark** for any one of the following ideas, or similar: • He is only four feet eleven inches tall, but he is a giant. • He is a giant. • Giants are not real.	1
2	**Award 1 mark** for next to the village	1
3	**Award 1 mark** for all three answers correct: the park, his house, his clothes	1
4	**Award 1 mark** for: To dry his eyes	1
5	**Award 1 mark** for both pairs of rhyming words matched correctly. cried – sighed groaned – moaned	1
6	**Award 1 mark** for: The people in the next village were complaining.	1
7	**Award 1 mark** for each plausible reason given, up to a maximum of **2 marks**, such as: • He thought he was very important. • He felt like an explorer. • He didn't have enough time to think of a name, so he used his own.	2
8	**Award 1 mark** for: Everything	1
9	**Award 1 mark** for all three answers correct. RAAAH a lot, terrify their villagers, eat cows	1
10	**Award 1 mark** for: splashed	1
11	**Award 1 mark** for a tidal wave.	1
12	**Award 1 mark** for: Four feet eleven inches	1
13	**Award 1 mark** for any one of the following ideas: • It is all right to be different and to not fit in. • Sometimes what we want isn't what we really want.	1
14	**Award 1 mark** for any reasonable answer, such as: • Oleg will return and be a proper giant. • Oleg will solve his problems and fit in again. • Oleg will never return.	1
15	**Award 1 mark** for inside Oscar's head / in his head	1
16	**Award 1 mark** for: alligator and elephant	1
17	**Award 1 mark** for any two of: mutter, squeak, squawk or jingle	1
18	**Award 1 mark** for all numbers correct. ① Oscar goes to sleep. ④ Oscar's Zoo disappears. ③ The animals have a feast. ② The Wallabear and Koalaby are in a tree.	1
19	**Award 1 mark** for any one of the following: the writer / the author / the poet / the person who wrote the poem / Graham Fletcher	1